Herman
the Hermit Crab
and
the Mystery
of the Big, Black,
Shiny Thing.

Sharon Canfield Dorsey
Author

Vivien B. Mann
Illustrator

High Tide Publications, Inc.
1000 Bland Point Road
Deltaville, Virginia 23043
www.HighTidePublications.com

Ordering Information: Quantity sales.

Special discounts are available on quantity purchases by corporations, associations, and others. For details, contact the "Special Sales Department" at the address above.

Illustrated by Vivien Mann
Printed in the United States of America

BISAC: Juvenile Fiction / Animals / Marine Life
ISBN-13: 978-1945990007

I dedicate this book
to my beautiful grandchildren,
Adaline, Emma, and Zachary,
who light up every day.

Herman, the hermit crab, awoke
and peeped out of his shell.

He looked up the beach.
He looked down the beach.

He crept closer to the edge
of the sea and looked all around.

There was seaweed, tiny pieces
of coral, lots of seashells,
and an old piece of sandy rope.

But none of his friends were there
- not Sammy the snail,
not Homer, his best hermit crab buddy,
not even Big John, the biggest and
smartest hermit crab on the beach.

Herman shifted
in his cramped shell.
He had outgrown his house.

He waddled across the sand,
looking for his friends.

Maybe they were resting
in the shade of
the Sea Grape Tree.

Herman was huffing and puffing
when he arrived at the trees.

There was Sammy and Homer
and lots of other hermit crabs,
all gathered around something big
and black and shiny.

"Homer, what is that?"
Homer shook his head.

"I don't know.
Maybe it's a big piece of
chocolate cake."

Chocolate cake was
Homer's favorite food.

Herman laughed.
"Sammy, what do you think it is?"

Sammy thought and thought.

"Could it be a new kind of house,
for a big hermit, like Big John?"

Herman didn't think so.

One wise old hermit thought
it might be a star that had
burned up and fallen from the sky.

A very young hermit wondered
if it was a turtle egg.

"Turtle eggs are white,"
Herman said in his kindest voice.

Quiet!
Do Not Disturb
I am Sleeping
Big John

The hermits kept moving closer,
circling the big, shiny thing.

There were big hermits
and middle-sized hermits
and little hermits
all lined up, watching.

Herman moved from
one hermit to another.
"Do YOU know what it is?"

They all shook their heads.

He came to the hermit closest to the
big, shiny thing.

It was Big John, the biggest
and smartest hermit on the beach.

Big John peeped a sleepy eye
out of his shell, and thundered,
"What are you
doing here?"

Herman crept closer.

"We're here to solve the mystery.
Is that why you're here?"

"I came to nap under the
Sea Grape tree."

It was very quiet.
The hermits waited.
They knew about Big John
and his grumpiness.

But Big John roared with laughter.

"Herman, you are the bravest
of all the hermits.
You must solve the mystery."

Herman didn't feel very brave at all.

Herman took a deep breath,
scurrying to the front, peeping at
the sides and under the back.

The big, shiny thing didn't move
or make a sound.

Herman clawed his way up the
side and fell back.

The Hermits watched,
cheering him on.

Herman was determined
to solve the mystery.

He climbed up again,
one last big push –

He was on top.

Herman began to laugh, and laugh.

The hermits moved closer.

"What is it? What is it?"

Big John smiled his biggest smile.

"I think Herman has
solved the mystery.
Tell them, Herman."

Sammy and Homer giggled.

"It's just an old oil bottle, washed up on the beach from a boat."

All the other hermits giggled too.

"Hooray for Herman!
Herman's our hero!"

Herman turned a happy, rosy pink.

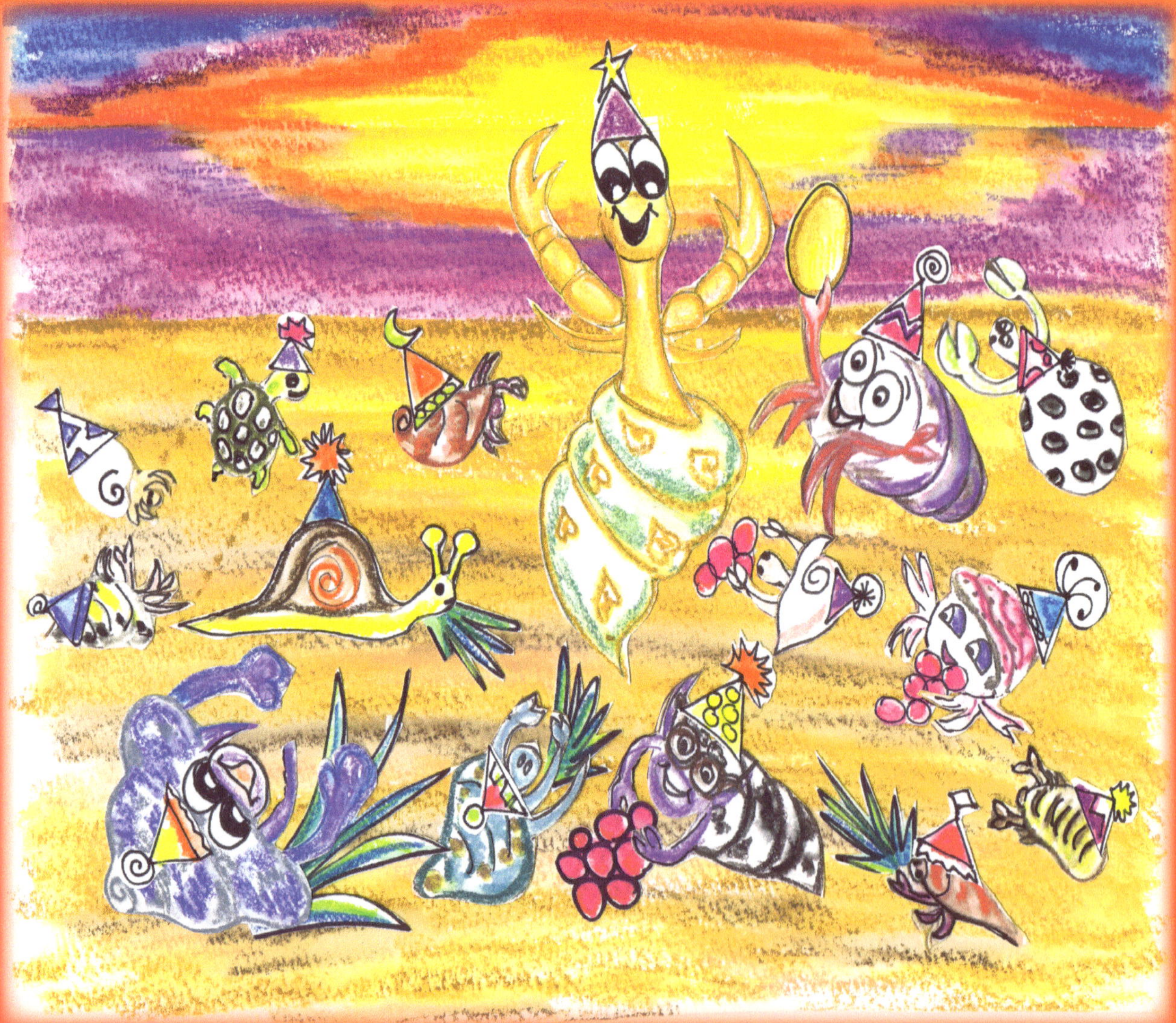

Big John had an idea.

"Let's have a party."

Sammy gathered sea grass and berries.

Homer found a potato chip.

Big John rewarded Herman with a new shell house.

And the hermits partied until the last golden ray of sun disappeared into the sea.

33

Other Books by Sharon Canfield Dorsey

Tapestry - Poems
Daughter of the Mountains - a memoir (due for release in 2017)

About the Author and the Illustrator

Vivien Mann and
Sharon Canfield Dorsey

Vivien B. Mann
Illustrator

Vivien is a mixed media artist and has exhibited her work in Arizona and Virginia. She enjoys painting, jewelry making and recycling "found" objects into interesting new creations.

As a social worker, providing support to children and young adults, Vivien has employed art as a tool to engage, promote self-awareness and healing, and just to have fun. Her work has taught her much about the resiliency of the human spirit. She is the mother of two children, Jenna and Matt, and several furry friends.

Sharon Canfield Dorsey
Author

Sharon is a member of the James City Poets and has received awards from the Poetry Society of Virginia, Chesapeake Bay Writers and Christopher Newport University Writer's Conference.

Her work has been published in magazines, journals, and anthologies. She has two children, Steven and Shannon, and three grandchildren, Adaline, Emma, and Zachary.

Sharon and Vivien are long-time friends. This is their first book collaboration

www.ingramcontent.com/pod-product-compliance
Lightning Source LLC
Chambersburg PA
CBHW060853270326
41934CB00002B/117